EDIT LIFE

TRANSFORMATION BEGINS WITH KNOWING THYSELF

MEGHANA KULKARNI

Copyright © Meghana Kulkarni
All Rights Reserved.

This book has been published with all efforts taken to make the material error-free after the consent of the author. However, the author and the publisher do not assume and hereby disclaim any liability to any party for any loss, damage, or disruption caused by errors or omissions, whether such errors or omissions result from negligence, accident, or any other cause.

While every effort has been made to avoid any mistake or omission, this publication is being sold on the condition and understanding that neither the author nor the publishers or printers would be liable in any manner to any person by reason of any mistake or omission in this publication or for any action taken or omitted to be taken or advice rendered or accepted on the basis of this work. For any defect in printing or binding the publishers will be liable only to replace the defective copy by another copy of this work then available.

For my mom and dad, with them in my life nothing can stop me from flying, thank you for being the wind beneath my wings!

Contents

Acknowledgements

The content of the book is solely meant to inspire and motivate the readers.

And it is the original work of the writer except for a few quotes that have been taken for inspirational purposes only.

Editing, Compiling, and illustration Work by Team WeTalk

Editing Work: Soorej Prasad

Preface

For 6 long years from 2014 to mid-2020 my life was a mess. I was moving in the wrong direction and had no crystalline purpose or goal in life. I was constantly stuck between pursuing my studies to running all across India for national competitions, life just kept on moving very fast without a pause, without a period of self-reflection. I was exhausted, stressed, anxious, and depressed and my mind flooded with never-ending thoughts of ending my life.

After all the exhaustion, in May 2020 I accidentally came across a book called **'The Beginnings' by Brahma Kumaris**. Little did I know that this book would lead me toward Inner transformation! While I am sorry for all those who lost their loved ones during the pandemic, for me personally, this period was a self-reflection phase, a wake-up call, and a spiritual awakening that eventually put me on a path toward inner transformation.

This book is a journey of my transformation, it's a reflection of who I was and whom I have become. You will understand why I call the dark phase of my life the miracle moments of my life. You will learn how a basic principle of a shift in perception can help you climb the transformation ladder upwards. But most importantly this book will help you re-think, if she can go through the pain and emerge stronger, so can I. If she can transform her darkness into light and spread love, so can I. If she can embrace her scars with pride, so can I. If she can share her authentic life story and inspire others, so can I. As humans, we all learn and evolve by understanding other people's failures, and adversities and how they overcame them. My message through this book is to help you understand that no matter what's going on in your life, you do have the courage and strength to face and overcome your adversities. That's where the strength and conditioning of your resilience muscle happens.

My only mission behind writing this manuscript is to help you re-think, that *if she can transform, so can I.* And I truly believe that we all have innate capabilities within us that can help us live a life beyond our wildest dreams. Fasten your seat belts, we are about to go on a roller coaster ride with Edit Life.

11 Filters – The First Step

Once I heard a speaker saying, *"A graveyard is a place filled with ideas...amazing ideas. All these highly intelligent beings with immense talent and creativity, they died with their hearts filled with regret, guilt, and shame. All these creative and well-crafted beings possessed million-dollar ideas but they never really executed them or probably gave up too early. Why? Because of FEAR!*

In April 2021, I had this great idea of writing a book and I procrastinated for nearly 10 months. It was not until Feb 2022, that I had a wonderful conversation with one of my friends who is also my mentor. As we were discussing various personal development topics, he paused and asked me an astonishing question, "Meghana, 6 months back you had told me about the idea of writing a book. How's it going?" I was numb and out of words. But this question got me into a deep-thinking state and finally, I answered "Well, it was just an idea. Nonetheless, I have been dreaming of writing a book for a long time, been getting universal nudges and signs to go for it but somehow, I have been procrastinating and somewhere, I think I am not ready or maybe the time isn't right. It's this weird confusion, my heart says go for it but my mind stops me every single time. Thus, I haven't put the thoughts into action". As he listened patiently, he raised another question, *"Well, what's stopping you from writing this 'ideal book'?* I thought for 5 minutes and then replied, "I think mainly its FEAR- fear of rejection, fear of failure, and the fear of uncertainty that's stopping me from taking action". There was a silence for 10 seconds, He then smiled and said, "When your heart saysgo for it, follow the old Nike cliché- *Just do it."* He imparted a pearl of very great wisdom to me that day about fear and intuition. He said, always remember, "*If it looks right and feels wrong, it's fear. If it looks wrong but feels right, it's your intuition.*" He added, "*Your longing to write a book has been your intuition telling you to go for it, but it's your ego that's stopping you every single time. It's time to shut down your ego and break another chain of fear by coming out of your comfort zone. Start writing and the answers will come to you. One step at a time, one thought at a time, one word at a time, one sentence at a time, one page at a time, one chapter at a time.*And finally, the birth of this book took place.

For me, it was my fear that was holding me back from writing this book. Once I changed my perception about fear, reprogrammed my mind, and got out of my comfort zone, that's where miracles started to happen. All it takes for you, is to come out of your comfort zone and then shift your perception and reframe your mindset in order to edit your life. That's where the real transformation journey begins.

You should be courageous enough to take the first step and trust where it leads

So, what's Edit Life all about?
TRANSFORMATION!

Most of the books talk about transformation and living a high-performance life. There is a famous quote that says, *"Don't let the entire staircase overwhelm you. Just focus on the first step"*. Thefirst step towards transforming life is to have a shift in perception. Its only when your perceptions shift positively, your mind starts noticing new patterns, new habits, new experiences and this eventually leads to the reprogramming of your mind. All you have to remember is, that if you want to transform your life, the first step is to shift your perception and reprogram your mind. How? Through unlearning and relearning certain aspects of your life.

This book is all about my perceptions and how a shift in perception has helped me deal with life. From being a failure in college, dealing with anxiety and depression, failing miserably in my sporting career to constantly raising questions to God asking, "Why me?" From being a clueless and directionless person Into a transformed person and the journey continues. Am I completely transformed? Hell no! Far from it. Nobody is 100% transformed. We are all work-in-progress beings. In this book, I share my low days, my most traumatic days and I also talk about certain topics which are mostly not taken too seriously as there is too much of content out there already. This book is not about right and wrong. This book is all about perceptions and how you can transform your life with the basic principle of "shift in perception". Every chapter, every filter in this book has its own flavor and authenticity linked to it. All you need to do is, have an open mind and a non-judgmental approach towards reading Edit Life.

I strongly believe if a person like me can shift my perceptions and manifest good luck into my life, so can you. Let my story inspire you to take action and transform your life. And who knows, one day you might share your authentic story that might inspire others to transform their life... you never know!

"TRANSFORMATION BEGINS WHEN THE DESIRE TO CHANGE IS GREATER THAN THE DESIRE TO REMAIN THE SAME"

CHAPTER ONE

Supernatural Power!

#gratitude #prayer #appreciation
#lifeisbeautiful #manifestation
#compassionate #intention
#perception #reframemind
#transformation #reprogramlife

One afternoon in June 2021, I received a text from one of my PUC (pre-university college) friends named Akshay Tarale, who is also a professional athlete. We were interacting after 4 long years. While we spent a couple of minutes sending formal texts and once the *friendship language* was back, I couldn't resist asking him about his sporting career, assuming he was still competing. Since we both come from a similar background and have a lot of commonalities, I finally raised the question, "Hey, are you still continuing with sports?" His immediate response was "Yup". Now he had all my attention. A person who pursued his engineering degree and still continuing with professional sports at the age of 24 seems unusual in a country like India. I responded by saying "That's amazing!

How often do we find players competing at a professional level after pursuing engineering? Hats off to you! Keep going man!" He responded saying "Thanks, but to be honest, the past few years have been really hard. I have had several injuries and unable to do a comeback. It's been more than 3 years that I am struggling. Working on my physiotherapy sessions, hoping I will do a comeback but looks like this injury is going to take some time and I'm not getting any younger. This is the most frustrating period of an athlete's life. I'm sure you can relate to this". When I received this text, I could sense the energy of what this person was going through. He was devastated, lost in life, filled with rage, his thoughts were filled with fear and negativity, and he sounded uncertain about his sporting career, moreover uncertain about his life. I explained to him about mindset and personal development that helped me transform my life. I immediately had an intense urge to get on a Zoom call with him and discuss the issues. By this time, I had built myself up confidently in terms of personal development and knew how mindset plays an important role in everybody's life. While I had no experience in mentoring, I had an intense urge to help this beautiful soul and I felt it's time to apply my knowledge and wisdom along with my 12+ years of sporting experience, all packed with the right intention. Two days later we got into a zoom call, discussed his issues, and he spoke his heart out. I made him do some visualization at the end of the session. After the call, I felt something different. The vibe I experienced was the joy of helping others. After all he was my 1st client and I was sure that this person is going to change and emerge stronger.

8 months later in February 2022, I spoke to him again and I see him as a completely different person. A

360-degree transformation. He had developed a positive attitude towards life and he was balancing his sporting life, financial life, and personal life. I was stunned to see this transformation and couldn't resist asking him, "8 months ago, you were all broken and at the lowest phase in your life. What happened to you? How did you transform your life?"

He said "Meghana, I am forever grateful for the session you took 8 months ago. It was an eye-opening talk for me. At the end of the visualization, you remember that I had tears rolling down my eyes and felt something very different. The words you spoke hit me so hard that it was like a wake-up call for me. For so many years, I was constantly blaming others for my failures. My thoughts were only towards those 100 people who were criticizing me rather than focusing on that handful of people who were uplifting me, even during my low days. When you spoke about gratitude and how one can change their thoughts and feelings, by focusing on the things we have rather than the things we don't have, this changed me as a person. This brought about a 360-degree transformation. Once I started practicing gratitude on a daily basis, I started to see that things were falling into place without any effort. Once I changed my thoughts and perception towards being grateful for all the little things in my life, that's where the magic happened". I was at a loss of words. My heart was filled with joy and once again, I thanked the universe for choosing me as an instrument to help others.

Living in a state of gratitude is the
gateway to grace

Being grateful for all the little things in life is a whole different experience altogether. Practicing gratitude is a miracle, and appreciating life, living life in the present moment, are no less than a miracle. When you thank God or the universe or your higher self or whichever superpower you believe in, they will provide you more in return. That's how the universe responds. All you need is to tune into something good that is going on in your life. Practicing gratitude, when you are low, can cheer you up. New doors will start opening up and new opportunities will start to manifest. You will see that there is a power greater than yourself that's taking care of you. Practicing gratitude, when you are happy and content, will help you connect to your higher-self and you will become a receiver of accurate intuitive answers. You may also experience ONENESS with your higher soul.

- Gratitude is a beautiful emotion.
- Gratitude is a form of prayer.
- Gratitude is a miracle.
- Gratitude is bliss.
- Gratitude is speaking your heart out.
- Gratitude is a way to communicate with a higher power.
- Gratitude is one's outlook towards life.
- Gratitude is going inward to know thyself.
- Gratitude is a superpower.
- Gratitude is key to attracting abundance.
- Gratitude is the key to manifestation.
- Gratitude is the key to living life beyond your wildest dreams.
- Gratitude is Everything.

If you can begin and end your day with the attitude of gratitude, there is no prayer that shall not be answered. There is no problem that can't be solved. The power lies in the word GRATITUDE. It could be as simple as – I am forever grateful to have wonderful supportive parents, I am grateful to have kind and compassionate friends by my side. Thank you so much for this beautiful day, thank you so much for the new opportunities and abundance, thank you so much for the constant flow of miracles in my life, etc. As G.E. Lessing quotes, *"One single grateful thought raised to heaven is the most perfect prayer."*

"GRATITUDE is a cocktail of right intention, positive emotions, speaking your heart out, and surrendering to the power that's greater than you. Gratitude means being grateful for every single thing in your life, EVERY SINGLE THING"

CHAPTER TWO

Be An Example!

#lifelessons #adversities #resilience
#mentalhealth #innerlight #innervoice
#miracles #perception #reframemind
#transformation #reprogramlife

In November 2017, my life had completely fallen apart. I had no faith, no hope and my mind was filled with never-ending thoughts of ending my life. I had no strength left in me anymore. I was helpless and the demon voice inside my mind insisted that *I stop suffering and put this to an end immediately.* That's where the irrational thought of ending my life rushed through me like a tsunami. I couldn't control myself, for I was not in control. *One late evening,* my body was numb, my mind was confused and my heart was completely frozen. *As* I was standing on the edge of my apartment terrace and was about to end my life, there were no thoughts or emotions running across my heart. For a moment, everything around me was paused and I couldn't feel anything. As I looked down, I made sure I would die and not be disabled for life. I looked up at the stars and felt nothing. I decided to close my eyes and jump so that I wouldn't see this disastrous world while I collapse. I closed my eyes and something miraculous happened. A beautiful calming inner voice said to me, **"BE AN EXAMPLE!"** The voice was loud and clear. As soon as I opened my eyes, my body was shivering out of fear and my mind was running at the speed of light. I felt like all of a sudden, I was alive again. As if someone had turned my life switch to ON. The time duration between me closing my eyes and the inner voice talking to me was about 5-8 seconds, I guess. I immediately got down and spent the next 3 hours sobbing on the terrace, trying to gather myself. I didn't know what that voice was trying to teach me or indicate to me, but all I knew was that the seed of hope was planted in me. I had been through a rough patch, the lowest point in my life for 6 long years. But this book is not a memoir. The reason I share this dark side of my story is for you to remember that when you are going through some rough times in your life or possibly your life has fallen apart, the light is still there. You may not understand the purpose of this light immediately but it is there. This light is a hope that "this too shall pass". My message to you, through my story, is that no matter what situation you are in, what failures you are going through or what journey you have embarked on, there is light and there is hope. Had I not listened to that inner voice, had I not seen the inner light guiding me, I wouldn't be writing this book today. As I continued my journey, trying to heal myself and embrace failures and social tantrums, I started to get closer to the sentence which meant, **"Be an example!"**.

Once you have healed yourself from the pain,

Make sure you light up the world

Today, I know what exactly this sentence was trying to teach me. It says, *"no matter what you are going through, let your failures be your strength, let your darkness be your light, let your scars be held with pride, for one day this shall be your strength and you will be set as an example to others"*. I understand that it's not easy to overcome failures. It's not easy to go through pain. I know your pain and I understand your pain. All I request, is that you believe that there is a hope, embrace this situation, and trust me, the universe will bless you with something that you couldn't have imagined. One day at a time, let the darkness fade away and let the pure light show you the direction and give you the strength so that you can heal and embrace your shame, guilt, and failures with pride and set an example to yourself and others.

I share this personal story, one of my dark sides, and my past with you so that you can remind yourself, *"Be an example"*. No matter which field you are in, no matter what failures you are going through, no matter what the future holds for you, sometimes you are the only one who can understand your battle. And this battle shall be your strength one day and the lessons you embrace shall be the memories you will cherish. So, friends, be an example. You don't have to be world-recognized to set an example. You could be an example within your family, within your friend circle, or your working profession, or something even bigger. The quantity doesn't really matter. All that matters is you pass on the torch and be an example in whatever you do, wherever you do it. Be a source of inspiration to others and your failures will be your strength one day.

Always remember, everyone has a story and everyone has a dark and bright side to their story. The person who understands and converts the dark into bright, will set the world on fire. Once you have healed yourself from the pain, make sure you become the fire. Make sure you share your failures with pride and make sure you pass on the torch to others with love and gratitude.

"When you let the inner light guide you, there is faith and hope. All you got to believe is that, you have a divine light within you. Surrender to this light and see the magic unfold in front of your eyes"

CHAPTER THREE

A Shift In Perception

*#attitude #thoughts #words #actions
#internalgrowth #growthmindset
#attitudeiseverything #perception
#reframemind #transformation
#reprogramlife*

Life is so boring!
Life is pathetic!
Life is terrible!
Life is full of shit!
Life is fucked up, ugh!

Now, you might be wondering why on earth would any self-help book start with a negative statement, right? When we look at our lives, we will find that 95% of the people we surround ourselves with are negative when life hits them hard. In 2021, when I was training a professional athlete for his mindset, I was patiently listening to his story and it was filled with lots of failures and hurdles. He was basically going through a crisis in his life. So, after listening to his story, I asked him a very obvious yet stupid question simply to hear his words aloud. I asked, "So, how do you feel about your life?" Now this young boy gave me a pathetic look and said "I just told you my entire story and how do you think I am feeling? My life is full of shit!" Now he had a shift in his emotions from feeling grief to frustration.

There is positivity in
every negativity,

there is hope in every
given situation

When we look at books written on attitude or when people in general talk about attitude, what they mean is **PERCEPTION**. The way you see and act towards a certain situation defines your attitude. Similarly in life, the way you think, the way you speak to yourself internally, the way you present yourself verbally, and the way you act when you are low is what determines your attitude. When your life is all happy, blissful, filled with miracles, winning all kinds of shiny trophies, you naturally have a positive attitude, right? But, what about when you are low? What about when life throws stones at you? What about when life throws you in the dirt from where you think you are unable to get up? What about when things are not working your way? What about when you fail? What about when someone breaks your heart? What do you think? What's the movie running inside your mind? What are the words you are constantly repeating to yourself? I understand that when you are low, finding solutions is difficult because when your emotions are high, your logic is low and you end up taking the worst decisions and putting yourself into more trouble. The best advice I give myself when I face a similar situation in life is, I tell myself to try to look at the positive side. There is positivity in every negativity, there is hope in every given situation but the real question is- *Are you ready to change your perception when you are low?* I am not talking about the positive change immediately but I am talking about a hope that says *"Wait a minute, what is this failure or situation trying to teach me? Is there anything else to it?"*. In these situations particularly you need to pay attention to your THOUGHTS. Most people will create melodrama inside their heads due to which they are unable to think clearly. The best way to conquer any negative situation or obstacles in your life is by developing a POSITIVE ATTITUDE. Once you start noticing positivity in every negativity, opportunities in every hurdle, and good in every bad, you start experiencing the outcome of the first step toward transformation which is – *a shift in perception*. Always remember- whatever you think and speak to yourself whenever life hits you hard, it WILL be manifested. Now I am not saying to ignore the hurdles and walk away, all I am saying here is to try to understand or analyze the situation from a positive perspective like – *what has this failure taught me? Why did I react irrationally towards a certain person? I accept the situation but what can I do NOW to change the reality?* The more frequently you ask questions, the deeper you go within yourself to find answers which eventually leads to building self-awareness. Daily reminder- A shift towards positive perception especially during LOW days can help you develop a positive attitude which leads to internal growth.

Remember, do not let one failure or thousands of failures determine your LIFE'S DEFINITION. Do not let criticism define your life. Do not let anyone else define your statement of life. What if I told you that irrespective of what you are feeling or going through, life is beautiful. Life is an amazing journey. All you need is to shift that mindset. No matter what happens in your life, life is beautiful. Don't let some pain define your life journey.

NURTURE YOUR MIND WITH GREAT
THOUGHTS

Next time you experience any sort of failure or pain in your life or perhaps things are not working your way, you might consider having a different approach towards the situation. All you need is HOPE and once hope is installed, the positive shift will occur automatically. Once your internal story changes, the external circumstances will change too. Once you change internally, that's when you will start observing the authentic beauty that lies ahead of you. *It's all about your thoughts, words and actions. If these 3 things are under your control, you will see life from a completely new perspective.*If you want to see positive changes externally, make sure you change your internal story first, that's where the magic is hidden.

"The way you think, the way you speak to yourself and others, the way you behave when you are feeling low or defeated is what defines your internal growth, it's all about perception, it's all about internal growth, PERIOD!"

CHAPTER FOUR

Know Your Definition

#success #failures #lifeisajourney
#resilience #mentaltoughness
#selfwareness #adversities #perception
#reframemind #transformation
#reprogramlife

Success and Failures are like two sides of the same coin. Imagine when you toss this "LIFE" coin up in the air, what do you hope for? Success, right? But life is a combination of success and failures. You have to taste failures in order to experience the joy of success and you have to taste success in order to experience the joy of failure. Before you jump to any conclusions and disagree saying *"how can there be any joy in failures?"* Ask yourself the last time you succeeded at something? Didn't you remember all your hard work, sacrifices, adversities and failures that helped you succeed? That's the joy of failure I'm talking about.

WHAT IS FAILURE?

Failure: This one word scares the shit out of people. And that's why most people do not act - because of the fear of failure. But if you try to zoom and get closer to this word, you will understand that most successful people in the world have failed thousands of times. Zoom a little bit more and you'll realize that you are not so unique because this word scares the shit out of everyone, even the world's most successful human beings. Understand this reality-*nobody likes to fail*, nobody likes to be seen as a failure and nobody likes to be criticized. NOBODY! Yet we all experience failures from time to time because it's a process. Failures are the stepping stone toward success and they are here to teach us some valuable lessons in life. **And there is nothing more victorious than failing.** The lessons you learn along the way, the emotions you experience when you fail. The constant rage going on in your mind when you fail, the feeling of not sure if you can ever do a comeback. The constant battle of giving up or trying one more time. The self-doubts, the low-confidence, fear of making a come-back, fear of taking a risk, fear of not knowing if you have strength left in you anymore to fight. Failure is going to squeeze you in all areas of your life and if you are lucky enough, all at once. Do not judge, just walk with me!

RELAX
The universe has your back

Failure will test your physical strength, your mental performance, your emotional stability, and your spiritual awareness. It will test you in all walks of your life - personal and professional life. From a relationship heartbreak to failing a business you thought you would succeed at. You will fail, you must fail, then you will learn, and then you must evolve. As a matter of fact, we all go through failures in our lives - just at a different time scale and at a different intensity. But we must remember that every situation has a bright side to it and so does failure. I like to look at failures as a long hideous dark tunnel and at the end of the tunnel, there is always the bright light that's waiting to show us a path, a direction, a hope, a sign that you fought well and you deserve peace and happiness.

Now you might ask me, *ok I get it, but what about the failures that keep constantly repeating in my life? How do I get rid of them?*

Failures are like a loop. Few things keep repeating in our lives. Same failures, again and again! That's what makes failure even more frustrating. When I imposed this question on one of my spiritual mentors he said, *"Similar failures will keep repeating in our lives if we do not learn and connect the dots from the previous failures. Ultimately, failure is here to teach us a lesson and help us grow, and if we fail to learn from failures, they seem to repeat"*. Makes sense!

Every failure teaches us something unique that's very much mysterious to us and it's our duty to connect the dots and learn from them. If you are aware of your failures and you have the willingness to address and accept the failures, you are already on a path towards inner transformation.

Now that you know the dark and the bright side of failure, your next question is quite obvious, *"how do I deal with failures?"*. Sorry to disappoint you but I'm not going to share 3 steps or 6 tricks to help you deal with failures. Rather, I'm going to share a very practical and spiritual answer with you. Always remember - *The universe would never give you anything that you cannot handle.* This statement alone should be enough for you to know that you do have the strength to face your failures.

"Failures are like a wake-up call in all areas of our life"

WHAT IS SUCCESS?

Success: As humans, we all are in the rat race towards success. Everybody wants it but the real question is, *"Are you really prepared for success?"*. There are tons of books, podcasts, YouTube videos, and theories that talk about success and each person shares their own perception of success. This word is intriguing and overwhelming at the same time. And if you have listened to my podcast, I begin the interview episode by asking the million-dollar question, *"What's your definition of success?"*. And what I observed is that, every single person has their own set of definitions and there is no such thing as right or wrong because each one of us lives differently, looks at life with different lenses, we are all unique species with unique definitions. Speaking of success and definitions, let me share my definition- **"Success to me is all about 1% growth every single day".** Let me decode this statement for you. We all grow and evolve due to our daily good habits and if we can become a better person by 1 % every single day, that contributes to a huge amount of success and growth. Conversely, you will face low days, long days and terrible days throughout the journey, and maintaining the 1% growth might seem as difficult as climbing Mount Everest. And during those days, all you need is consistency. Even if that means staying in the same percentile zone. All that matters is that you don't give up, hang in there and continue to play the game.

Let me share one of my personal stories to help you wrap your head around this statement. I have been meditating consistently since mid-2020. There have been days when I was excited and ready for meditation and experienced the best of spiritual practices. But there have also been days when my mind was filled with never-ending thoughts, my heart was filled with fear and I felt that I shouldn't sit for meditation when I am extremely disturbed psychologically and emotionally. That's where the consistency kicks in. Although mental and emotional disturbance didn't let me achieve the highest state of peace and calmness, it did teach me the importance of consistency. I understand that not all days are the same. Sometimes you have intense energy and confidence that makes you feel you can climb Mount Everest and some days are boring and gloomy, making you feel you can't climb a flight of stairs and it's OK! ***Sometimes it's 1% growth every day and sometimes it's maintaining consistency every day.*** That's where success lies. That's where success tests you, that's where success plays tricks on you. The way you look at success is going to define your success curve in life.

Now, I want you to define, what's your definition of success?

"*Success to me is all about <u>1% growth</u> every single day*"

CHAPTER FIVE

Tragedy Before Transformation

*#lifelessons #innergrowth #evolve
#resilience #darkphase #lowestpoint
#miracles #perception #reframemind
#transformation #reprogramelife*

For 70 months of my life, I was clueless, directionless, and helpless. From August 2014 to June 2020, I experienced a dark phase of my life. Every day seemed like a struggle. While I was smiling and enjoying life, it was quite the opposite. I was lost, filled with rage, had no direction in life, and got consumed with negativity. I was at the lowest point in my life. Being an electrical engineer, experiencing the ups and downs of college life. I had accumulated double-digit backlogs as I had no interest in attending boring lectures. My health turned reversal on me, and the hostel food impacted my health due to which I was admitted to the hospital once every 2 months. My sporting career started to fall off the cliff, I had injuries onc after another and in most of the nationals, I couldn't even qualify to the main draw. My personal life had fallen apart as well. I barely spoke to my parents, I had created fake friends and started partying, bunking classes, and enjoying my so-called fake life to the fullest. For 6 long years, I had been experiencing stress, anxiety, depression, and suicidal thoughts. I had created my own world inside my imaginary mind and I failed myself every single day. All the decisions I made led to consistent failures. I felt helpless and was unaware that I was heading in the wrong direction. I constantly blamed others for my failures. It took me 6 long years to realize that I had been depressed and unhappy about everything in my life. This realization hit me so hard that I promised myself that I will heal and come back stronger. HOW? The universe speaks in mysterious ways!

In 2020 when the world shut down, we all were given a chance to re-program our lives. I decided to take control of my life. 100% responsibility. I started to re-access my life and started questioning every single thing that occurred during 2014-2020. I spent several months journaling, self-discovering, and understanding my failures. I started meditating and reading self-help books. After 8 months of exploring my failures, I did find changes in my behavior and thought patterns and my outlook on life was certainly changing or heading towards positivity. I can't describe it in words but I did experience happiness after a long time. For all my years, I used to yell that 2014-2020 have been the worst years of my life. Today, I proudly re-frame the statement as **"2014-2020 have been the best years of my life"**. The life lessons I learned are countless. I am proud and lucky to have been through this tragedy, the best phase of my life. I am grateful for those dark days, the struggle, the constant thought of quitting or even suicidal thoughts. I am grateful for all those hours of sobbing and not knowing what to do in life. Today when I share my story with people and they ask me the obvious question-

"If you had the chance to go back and change your life, would you ever change anything?".

My immediate response is, "HELL NO!", because...

- *I am grateful for those lowest moments in my life- they taught me who I am. They made me strong and wise. Forever grateful.*
- *I am grateful to have stayed in a hostel, away from home. I am grateful to have fallen sick regularly-these experiences taught me to value my physical health and taught me self-care, self-love, and self-appreciation. Forever grateful.*
- *I am grateful for all the professors who criticized me, all the people who didn't believe in me, everyone who was ashamed of having me in their life- this taught me the most important lesson in life, the lesson of ego-shattering. These are the people who gave me an opportunity to go within myself to find answers. Today I am a self-aware person and I wouldn't go back and change a single thing. Forever grateful.*
- *I am grateful for all the backlogs, education failures, and tantrums that I experienced along the way. It taught me who I am, what I am passionate about, showed me what I like and dislike and showed me the direction in life. If I hadn't been directionless for years together, if I hadn't failed and accumulated backlogs, today I wouldn't have had a direction in life. I wouldn't be following my soul purpose. Forever grateful.*
- *I am grateful for all the injuries I had to face, the constant failure in my sporting career. If not, I wouldn't know the real reason behind my failure, which was clearly the lack*

of a positive mindset. It's because of these failures that I started studying human behavior, mindset and got into personal development programs. Forever grateful.

- I am grateful to have experienced stress, anxiety, depression and even suicidal thoughts. They taught me to value life, appreciate life, show empathy and so much more. Forever grateful.

- I am grateful for all my fake friends, all the partying and bunking classes- they taught me what a delusional life looks like. Today I can differentiate what is fake and what is wise. I am wise enough to know if someone is trying to sugarcoat me or is trying to stab me behind my back. Forever grateful.

EVERY TRAGEDY LEADS TO A BEAUTIFUL DESTINATION

If I had to summarize one thing that these 6 long years of tragedy and miracles taught me, it was "INNER STRENGTH" or you can call it "RESILIENCE". Someone said it well- **You never know how strong you are until being strong is the only option you have.**

If you are going through a similar situation in life, if you are experiencing defeat in some or most of the areas of your life, if you feel your life is falling apart and constantly digging for the answers from God asking "Why me?", then know that this is your test period. Because every tragedy leads to a beautiful destination. Remind yourself - this too shall pass. You may not understand this immediately but one day you will look back and say that these incidents or failures changed your life. *Remember: The universe will never give you anything that you cannot handle.* Let it be an accident or a death of a family member or failure to crack your MBA entrance exam or a breakup or even a near-death experience. Whatever you are going through, know that it will pass, it should pass. Once you have learned the lesson and are ready to evolve and move ahead in life, believe me, the universe will place a magical door in front of you. Once you have passed your tragedy test, you will see the transformation.

Always remember – *Tragedy leads to building Resilience and Resilience leads to Inner Transformation.*

"*Tragedies are like invisible miracles- they keep a track of your RESILIENCE. Once you surpass the tragedy test, emerge stronger and wiser, that's when the miracle door opens up, that's where TRANSFORMATION begins*"

MEGHANA KULKARNI

CHAPTER SIX

Surviving or Living?

#living #surviving #livelife #enjoy
#beyou #beunique #bestversion
#perception #reframemind
#transformation #reprogramelife

Back in the day when I was pursuing my studies and managing sports, life seemed more like a struggle. Every single day when I went to bed, I used to stare up at the roof and ask myself just one question, "What am I doing?" I was rushing to college, rushing to play badminton, partying hard and life seemed to be moving very fast but in the wrong direction. I wasn't happy with myself and thus I felt my life was a struggle. Little did I know something called surviving? For all my college days, I was surviving every single day not knowing what next, not knowing where my life was heading towards. I felt like a lost person in the crowd of other lost people all moving in the similar direction. Every single night before I shut my eyes, this particular thought bothered me, *"What am I doing in life? Why am I doing this?"* **I felt an intense negative emotion**

rush through my heart every time I raised this question. It was a negative feeling of surviving in an uncomfortable nutshell. Fast-forwarding my life today, every night I go to bed, I look up at the roof and ask myself the similar question as to, *"What am I doing in life? Why am I doing it?".* These are the thoughts that run across my mind before I shut my eyes from this physical world. This time, my emotions are positive. I feel my heart expand with joy and gratitude every time I raise this question today. Why? **Because I am *living* positively in an uncomfortable nutshell.** The only difference between the older version and the new version is that, today I am following my dreams, my goals and my passion. I do things that make me happy and sets my soul on fire. Back in the day, I was studying subjects I was least interested. I lost my momentum in life because I wasn't enjoying what I was doing and when you do not enjoy what you are doing, you are in the survivor mode of your life. Life is uncomfortable irrespective of the survivor or living mode. The only difference is that the living mode gives you the strength and courage to face these uncomfortable moments.

As Steve Jobs had once said, *"If today were the last day of your life, would you want to do what you are about to do today?"* This question intrigued me and since then I have been asking myself a similar question, every day I wake up. Do some spiritual practices like getting out of my bed, looking at myself in the mirror and asking a similar question in a more fashioned way, "Am I surviving or living?"

Speaking of surviving,

1) Surviving is waking up every day and following a monotonous life.

2) Surviving is helping others live their dreams at the cost of your own dreams.

3) Surviving is trying to please everyone around you.

4) Surviving is not standing up for yourself when it's needed the most.

5) Surviving is living life without any purpose or direction.

6) Surviving is listening to others' decisions rather than your inner voice.

7) Surviving is when you make someone else the top priority at the cost of your own well-being.

8) Surviving is not living the life that is true to yourself.

9) Surviving is not living the authentic person you are.

10) Surviving is the sacrifice you make at the cost of your emotional well-being.

I can go on and on and list another 50 points but I'm sure you get my point.

"Surviving is the drug you consume every single day which is affecting every single area of your life".

We are humans, the highest form of God's creation. We have the highest form of intellectual understanding of ourselves and the environment. Yet, we keep consuming these "surviving pills" every single day. No wonder humans are the only species who experience stress, anxiety and depression. But, as a human race, we are all in the pursuit of happiness and the key component of happiness is LIVING.

Living is all about exploring the
different flavors of life

Speaking of living,

1. Living is enjoying every moment of life.
2. Living is to express the authentic you to the world.
3. Living is in the present moment.
4. Living is taking moderate or slightly higher risks in life.
5. Living is being spontaneous.
6. Living is being a little crazy and getting adventurous.
7. Living is zero expectation policy.
8. Living is following your dreams and passion.
9. Living is getting out of the comfort zone and creating your own destiny.
10. Living is trying different flavors of life.

I hope by now you understand the major difference between these two words. Your entire life is revolving around these 2 words. You have a choice, surviving mode or living mode. Perhaps you have a whole different philosophy on this topic. It doesn't matter. All that matters is when you wake up tomorrow morning and see yourself in the mirror, just ask yourself,

1) Am I surviving or living?

2) If I'm surviving, what can I do to make the best possible changes to suit my current situation?

3) If I'm living, what can I do to maintain consistency so that I can experience bliss every moment of my life?

"Surviving or Living is the choice you make."

CHAPTER SEVEN

The Only Secret to Success

*#success #determination #dedication
#discipline #consistency #patience
#selfawareness #perception
#reframemind #transformation
#reprogramlife*

In March 2021, a rush of adrenaline was flowing all across my body. By this time, I had crossed 8 months of the 'self-discovering phase' and was high on personal development. All my life I had heard people talk about personal development and how it can change a person's behavior and lifestyle. Today, I was experiencing 50% of what these people were trying to convey. I was high on self-help books and my determination to change my life started growing rapidly. My life revolved around self-transformation. Surprisingly, the people I met, the advertisements I saw on digital platform, it was all about personal development, mindset and spirituality. One advertisement on YouTube grabbed my attention in particular. It was a 3-day online event. The main theme of the entire program was "How to become successful". Almost thousands of books talk about success and failures, and I had read dozens of them myself, but nonetheless, I was interested to know more, always hungry for more even when my brain exploded saying "Mental Virus". Thus, I attended this personal development mastermind program.

Today, if we look at digital advertisements or if you read a lot of books on personal development, everyone talks about how to become successful. When I saw this advertisement for the 1st time, I immediately signed up for the program without giving a second thought. Why? Because like any of you, I was in search of those mantras to become successful. The word success itself is a magical word that can blow away anybody's mind because we all want to be successful, whatever the definition of success means to you. If you know me, I'm an avid reader and have spent 8 months of my life only reading, listening to podcasts, and exploring different things in life until I found a clear goal or mission in life. Every book I read, every podcast I listened to, had its own flavor of expressing or I would like to say had its own perception about how to achieve certain things in life. When I attended this 3-day mastermind program, I expected I would find a 6-step process in order to achieve success. But to my surprise what I found was an eye-opening and practical approach to becoming successful. This is where I learned the 3-D model of success.

Before I explain the 3D model, let me remind you of something right away. It doesn't matter where you are in life right now, it doesn't matter which profession you choose, it doesn't matter what your personality looks like and your past failures don't count anymore. All you need is A GOAL. Once you are aware of where your talent and creativity lie and want to pursue further in a similar direction, that's a goal. It's a direction to head towards. Once you find a goal or target, then it's time to apply the secret ingredients. It's time to apply the 3-D model.

- DETERMINATION.
- DEDICATION.
- DISCIPLINE.

DETERMINATION IS ALL ABOUT PUSHING BEYOND YOUR LIMITS

DETERMINATION: This word denotes to me, "If it can be done, it will be done. If it cannot be done, it will still be done." When I spent 8 months exploring myself, I came to the conclusion that I needed to help others with my knowledge and wisdom. While I was clear on doing something in sports but unsure of the particular subjects, I was determined enough to dive deep into the sports field and explore various options and see which fits best for me.

In life, it is similar, if you have a goal in front of you, it's a destination you want to reach. But what about the process? How are you going to do it? What's the strategy? That's where the determination creeps in- you need the determination to find out, to figure out the process or strategy, to dive deep into the roots or the core of your goals and understand how you going to do it. Determination is all about getting your ass off the couch and finding a way out. Do some out-of-the-box thinking and find a way to make it happen. If you're an athlete and you set your goal towards achieving an Olympic medal, be determined enough to go through the process. Be determined enough to find out every single error in order to achieve that goal, be determined enough to pay attention to every single detail. Be determined enough to enjoy the process.

"DETERMINATION IS ALL ABOUT PUSHING BEYOND YOUR LIMITS, it's all about staying hungry in order to make your dream come true."

It's all about failing consistently
UNTIL THE WORLD LOOKS AT YOUR SUCCESS AS AN OVERNIGHT REWARD

DEDICATION: It's all about consistency. Dedication is delivering results every single day. When I was on the path toward exploring myself, I felt like quitting several times because I didn't see any progress happening and I felt like I was moving backward than moving forward. As James Clear, the famous author, writes in his book Atomic habits, *"Some changes often appear to make no difference until you cross a critical threshold. The most powerful outcomes of any compounding process are delayed. You need to be patient"*.Staying patient and being consistent is what dedication is all about. In life, most people give up thinking it's not working for them or the goals seem too unrealistic. In reality, they are very close to achieving their goals. I have met dozens of athletes who were talented, hardworking, had great national rankings and a huge dream to represent India and make it big. But 5 tournaments they don't perform and they start believing that their hard work is not paying off. If 5 tournaments define your failures, if 1 year of non-performance defines your life, then what about people who have become successful overnight? If you listen to their stories, they have failed consistently for years together to make it look like an overnight success. If you are working hard towards your goals, you have a burning desire within yourself, you have a determination muscle and that is all you need to do is keep going. Never give up!

> *"DEDICATION IS ALL ABOUT BEING PATIENT AND maintaining CONSISTENCY. It's all about FAILING CONSISTENTENLY UNTIL the world looks at your success as an overnight reward"*

Discipline
IS AN ATTITUDE

DISCIPLINE: Discipline is an attitude. It's a way of thinking and behaving. Discipline is going the extra mile when you feel you can't go. Discipline is showing up when you feel you have no energy left in you anymore. It is all about actions. When you have a big goal in front of you, not all days are going to be similar. Some days you give your 100% and some days are the so-called *not your days*. Discipline is all about what you do when you are facing "not your days". If you are on a strict healthy diet and one day you crave a dessert, the disciplined person is the one who has the ability to say NO to the dessert that is kept in front of him/her even on the days when the craving for dessert is optimal. Discipline is self-awareness. It's the capability of saying NO when you badly want to yell by saying YES and vice versa. It's all about knowing what's right and wrong for you. It's all about the goal in front of you. It's all about the actions you take every single day in order to get 0.0001% close to your goals.

> *"DISCIPLINE IS ALL ABOUT SAYING NO WHEN THE MONSTER INSIDE YOUR HEAD IS YELLING YES, IT'S ALL ABOUT SELF-AWARENESS"*

By now you might realize that there is no secret sauce for success. You can't follow a single recipe and assume you will become successful. No matter the dish you want to cook, no matter the recipe you want to make, all you need is the major ingredients to make your dish more delicious. And these are the major ingredients when it comes to real life and success. I'm not against a success model or 6 steps formulae. All that is great but you need a strategy in life. And you can't cook a delicious dish by using all the ingredients in the same quantity, can you? In fact, every dish has major ingredients that spice up its deliciousness.

"*DETERMINATION, DEDICATION AND DISCIPLINE are the major ingredients that can spice up the deliciousness of success*"

CHAPTER EIGHT

Perfectly Imperfect

*#perfectionism #overthinking
#authenticity #beyou #ownyourstory
#inspireothers #bestversionofyourself
#perception #reframemind
#transformation #reprogramelife*

When I began the journey of writing this book, it was all exciting and thrilling. I enjoyed daydreaming of writing the book, the feeling of paper scent, visualizing the cover picture and the impact it would create in the world. Little did I know that this feeling wouldn't last forever and soon I was worn out of excitement. That's when the gloomy days began. I knew my purpose behind writing this book but sometimes in life, you get caught up in the internal drama so much that you don't realize there are a thousand steps ahead of you. As I started writing daily, I devoted 2 hours for self-exploration and dug deep into my mind to gather all the things that have occurred over a period of time that has helped me change my perspective. In the beginning, I had a very chill *know it all attitude*. When I sat down at my desk, I stared for 'N' number of hours at the screen of my laptop, waiting for the innovative thoughts to pour into my head and onto my fingertips to help me type this inspiring manuscript. I was filled with fear, the thought of imposter syndrome filled up my mind. When I spoke about this to one of my friends who had experienced similar issues while writing his 1st book, he understood my root problem and immediately responded saying, "*Meghana, I think you are way too focused on the outcome rather than the process*". Now, this is the phenomenon I keep telling everyone to follow. In fact, I have followed it for years together and have experienced some marvelous results. This time, I was caught up in the internal drama and as soon as my friend spoke those words out, I felt an intense energy flow down my spine. I became aware and I realized that it was time to replace this "outcome-based" hat with the "enjoy the process" hat. I immediately shifted my perception and reframed my mindset by reminding myself to enjoy the process. I even created an attractive sticky note that said "ENJOY THE PROCESS".

The one that is most personal
is the most creative

When I was at the very beginning stage of putting this manuscript together, I had a vision of sharing my thoughts, my perception and how I reprogrammed my life. I was ready with all the kick-ass inspiring quotes, book recommendations and notes from past 2 years of journaling. But to be honest, something didn't seem right. I sensed that there was no clarity about my internal motivation for writing this book. Thus, I battled every single day. There were days when I felt that writing this book was the most stupid thought that has ever occurred in my life. The constant battle with imposter syndrome and the negative bitch inside my head that was always trying to pull me down. I was so frustrated and constantly searching for answers. I was aware that I needed to enjoy the process, but I was not enjoying it. And the worst part, I was very hard on myself because I was in search of perfectionism. Speaking of perfectionism, I was demanding myself to write the best book, the perfect book. A book that would gain all the adorations in the market. I was caught up in this internal drama and the day I became aware of this melodrama, I decided to pray. That's the only solution you have. When you can't get the answers from external sources or from your conscious mind, it's time to pull the higher cards. Ask your inner self, the wise one, the higher soul for guidance.

On 16th May 2022, the full moon day, which was an auspicious day, also celebrated as Wesak, we had a group mediation at our spiritual center and each one of us had to write down our wish list on a piece of paper and hand over to the "miracle basket" before the meditation started. Few minutes into the group mediation, all of us were into the deep meditative state, the energies felt strong and blissful. That's exactly when I heard 4 different voices inside my head hovering, BE AUTHENTIC, BE YOURSELF, WRITE YOUR STORY, SURRENDER.

After the meditation ceremony, I had all the answers to my questions regarding the book. Earlier, I was writing the book in a very conceptual format- just sharing my ideas, thoughts, and perception and had very little to do with my life story. Worse, I was not being authentic. I was trying to be someone else. I wasn't ready to share my personal story due to which I was unable to enjoy the process. More importantly, I was trying to be perfect. It was only when I combined my authentic personal stories and experiences with my ideas, thoughts and perceptions that I started to enjoy the journey. I experienced my thoughts running at the speed of light and my fingers moving faster than usual. I did experience a lot of internal battles and emotional turbulence while sharing my personal stories. After all, it's not that easy to recollect or relive a past memory that affected your well-being. I knew one thing- I had to share my true story, my personal stories, to help you realize that you are not alone in this journey called LIFE. I reminded myself daily - *when I share my authentic imperfect stories, I am healing myself...I am healing a part of me that is undiscovered.*

Live a life that's true to
yourself and the show will last
forever

We hear a lot of people talk about "be the best version of yourself" or "be the authentic you" or "just be yourself". What they are really trying to say is- when you try to be who you really are, at the core of your heart, the crazy you, the authentic you, the imperfect you, the unusual you, the undiscovered you, that's when you can impact other people and that's where you start enjoying the process and journey. When you try to mimic others, try to be someone you are not and your energy will tell everything about yourself. Worse, you are not true to yourself and you do not want to do injustice to yourself.

A daily reminder: Each one of us is different. We are a unique family of species. The way we think, speak and act is also different. The way we experience and perceive things in life is also different. We are not the same and that's why each one of us is unique in our own authentic way. **Discover who you really are, be yourself, and do not try to mimic anyone. Live a life that's true to yourself and the show will last forever.** We are all beautifully crafted and are perfectly imperfect and so let it be that way. It's the hidden imperfection that brings out the best version of you".

"Your true authenticity lies in being honest with yourself, lifting the mask up and breaking the internal walls of perfectionism, because we all are PERFECTLY IMPERFECT"

CHAPTER NINE

Battlefield

*#life #dreams #struggle #miracles
#lonely #faith #resilience #perception
#reframemind #transformation
#reprogramlife*

October 2020 was the 'discovering' phase of my life. During this phase, I was just observing and analyzing everything around me. The books I read, the courses I enrolled for, the podcasts I consumed on a daily basis and the people I associated with. Most importantly, I was keenly observing my thought patterns and emotional stability. Now you might be wondering who would waste so much time only in observing and analyzing, right? Well to be precise, there are few crazy people like me. And the outcome of this phase was quite astonishing. I was observing and understanding not just myself but everyone around me. I have spent weeks together, just observing and understanding. I used to practice journaling, understand why people behave in a certain way. Why they did what they did. From a 2-year-old baby to a 75-year-old grandmother, I was observing and creating patterns about each one of them. Within several months, my observing and understanding skills grew rapidly and soon I started to predict every move of all the people I had known and observed. I felt an intense urge to get into various psychological courses or programs. As the number of Covid cases started to spike up exponentially, so did my thirst for knowledge and wisdom grow rapidly. While I enjoyed every single day of self-exploration, trying to wrap my head around all these psychological concepts, I developed a new interest in the field of psychology, personal development and spirituality. I thought of pursuing my higher studies in the respective domains. Although I come from an engineering background, I made a decision to pursue my master's in sports psychology. To my surprise, very few universities did provide a master's in sports psychology for students who did not hold an undergraduate degree in psychology. While I was busy doing my research and found that most of the UK universities did allow engineering students to pursue their masters, I set my intention to fly to the UK for higher studies. I started studying for IELTS and applied for the exams. While all this was great, I felt I needed help in choosing one from the various universities. I contacted a nearby career counselor (this was purely my intuition, guiding me to seek help). As I met the counselor, he patiently listened to my 6 long years of education drama and the new passion that I had developed. He finally suggested me to take a test. He introduced me to something very different called as a "Psychometric test". Never did I hear about this test in my entire life and here I was, giving a 3-hour test. Psychometric test is an artificial intelligence (AI) based test, which reveals everything about your personality, your interests, logical reasoning, and verbal understanding. Basically, it helps an individual choose a career in life that goes with his talents, personality, passion and so much more. Once my results were out, to my surprise, I had 10 different top choices, 20 different good choices and 10 different optional choices. I was stunned by these results and by God's grace, Srinivas sir, who was my career counselor, asked me various questions, gave me some elderly advice and told me to take a wise decision. He said, *"Always remember that whenever you take a decision in life, listen to your heart and not your mind".* This session was an eye-opener for me. I had been there to select one from the various UK universities for my higher education and here I was, with a completely new career choice. The universe does speak in mysterious ways. I instantly dropped the plan of pursuing a master's degree. The reason I had chosen masters in sports psychology was due to my 12+ years of experience in sports and also having been a victim of anxiety and depression. I couldn't resist anyone suffering from mental health issues and I badly needed to extend my hand to help them. After all, my mission is to inspire and help others in any way possible. Then I remembered my mentor's words, "You don't particularly need a degree to help others, you just need a pure and loving intention". Dropping the plan of pursuing a master's degree was very difficult. It was a gut feeling, an intuitive answer, a call from the universe and you never play around with your intuitive answer. I believed that there was something more in store for me and I couldn't wait to discover this whole new mysterious journey.

Universe will test you before it places amazing people into your life

One afternoon in February 2021, I sat with my dad and explained to him my dreams and goals. Of course, the dreams and goals were not 100% crystal clear but I could see the direction of my ship sailing towards something big. I told my dad, *"I am keenly interested in psychology and human behavior. I have found a new path of personal development and have a good understanding of how mindset works. I want to share my knowledge and experience with the rest of the world so that they can benefit from it. I am going to start with YouTube and podcasting, as a source to help humanity"*. As you must know, my dad was not like a Hollywood cool dad who would say, "Wow, this sounds interesting". So, I looked at him and asked, "What do you think, dad?" There was confusion written all over his face. I could sense his fearful energy and insecurities creep in. He was stunned and at the same time ready to give me a lecture on "You are choosing the wrong direction. You should go for a stable job and a stable lifestyle. Why do you want to play a high-risk game in life at this stage?" He didn't use these exact words but I am sure that this is what was going on in his mind. After all, if you come from an engineering family and have great observational skills, you eventually learn to predict their every move. And it's not difficult to predict Indian parents. They somehow have similar genes of saying "stable job, stable lifestyle". I followed my heart and started sharing whatever I knew through YouTube and podcasts. Meanwhile, I also started speaking to various professional athletes, understanding their issues and combining my sports experience and knowledge, I helped them in whatever way possible.

The reason I am sharing my personal story with you is, when I started my journey with a vision and big dream ahead of me, it was lonely and dark. I didn't know where to go, whom to approach and how to start. I just knew I had to inspire and share my experience and knowledge with the world. And what I learned was remarkable. Often, a lonely journey leads to a beautiful destination. For 6 months, I was all alone fighting my battles against the world. And in no time, one friend joined me on my mission. 4 months later, another mate joined my mission. 6 months later, I had 15 new people who believed in my mission and were guiding me towards the right goals. And the army keeps expanding till today.

Sometimes in life, you have a goal, a desire, and a mission that is so powerful and close to your heart that it makes sense only to you. The rest of the world will criticize you, throw harsh negative comments on you and they will try to pull you apart from your dream and vision. A few might leave you, a few might hate you, a few might be jealous of you and many of them will advise you not to go for it because it seems impractical or beyond your reach. They advise you to be realistic. But the truth is, this is your dream, it's visible only to you and it's been installed only in you for a reason. Life will test you with this big dream, you might feel like it's you against your demons and if you can conquer your demons and overcome the fear, the universe will respond to your actions. All you need to do is, pick up your sword confidently and the universe will place an army behind you and soon you will realise that you are not alone on this battlefield, your soul mission.

Today I can proudly say that I did overcome my initial fears and embraced all my scars with pride and that's how the universe placed amazing people into my life who are constantly guiding me.

If you are going through a rough patch in your life and are feeling lonely on your journey, know that you have all the strength and courage to face life. Let life test you before it can place amazing things and people into your life and your journey won't seem lonely anymore. You will have an army of people supporting you, guiding you and taking care of you. For now, all you need to do is, follow your heart, for it knows what your soul mission is all about. And if you can't hear what your heart is saying to you, all you need to do is ask, **"What is my soul mission in this lifetime?"** Meditate upon this question and let the answers flow to you whenever you are ready to receive. Always remember,

- ASK AND IT SHALL BE GIVEN.
- SEEK AND YE SHALL FIND
- KNOCK AND IT SHALL BE OPENED UNTO YOU.

> *"In Life, the quantity of your army doesn't matter. If you have a handful of positive mindset people beside you, there is no one who can stop you from building an empire or creating history. Always choose quality over quantity, positive over negative and real over fake."*

CHAPTER TEN

Just Explore

*#explore #selfawareness #enjoylife
#wanderlust #funalongtheway #passion
#likesanddisalikes #perception
#reframemind #transformation
#reprogramlife*

When I was 10 years old, people often asked me what I aspired to become in the future and my immediate response was- a model. At 15 years of age, my response changed to becoming a cardiologist. At 18 years of age, my response changed to an Olympic gold medalist, and today, when people ask me what I aspire to be, I respond by saying, an **EXPLORER.**

If we observe our life, it is strange to see the life curve and how the responses change over the course of time. Today when parents come to me and ask, "Should I enroll my kid in badminton or athletics? Should he get into cricket or swimming? Should he pursue science or arts? Should he become a doctor or an engineer or a lawyer?" These are the confusing questions every parent has in their mind. My answer is very simple, "Let them explore life". Let the child get an opportunity to play various sports, explore various career options, and see where he or she finds their strength and passion. **Life is all about learning and exploring and not reaching a particular destination, because there is always more to life.** Who knows, the kid might find 2-3 sports exciting or maybe he or she just doesn't incline towards sports and is attracted to mathematics. Don't try to force anyone, let them explore. When you explore, you learn. When you learn, you understand various patterns. When you understand various patterns, you analyze life and once you start analyzing life, you become self-aware. In order to become self-aware about your likes and dislikes, you must **first explore**.

For me the journey of exploration started at a very young age and I am forever grateful to a beautiful soul in my life, my mother, who enrolled me in various activities throughout my developmental stages. Before I chose badminton as a professional sport, I played and competed in various sports (though not professionally). My mother motivated me to participate in all cultural activities...dance, singing, elocution, debate, acting, you name it and she had in on her mind already! She had taken me to a few movie auditions back in the day and thus I developed the craze of becoming a model one day. Every time I participated in any activity, I wanted to win. I wanted the shiny trophies, the glorious medals and a file filled with overflowing certificates. But my mom reminded me of one thing, she said, ***"Just go and enjoy Manu(my nickname)"***. She made sure that I was well prepared for the events and that I enjoy the process as well. Today, when I look back at my life and acknowledge all my Bharatnatyam certificates or when I recall my debate competitions, I realize one thing -

I may not have won all the competitions but it surely has made me a confident person today. All the talents, gifts, and creativity that I possess today, are the result of doing these little things in life that over a period of time make you a whole different person, without your acknowledgment. *Life is all about exploring, see where you find joy and happiness and do not settle for anything less than you deserve.*

Life is all about exploring
It's a girl

When it comes to choosing a sport, a career, a job, a life partner, a vacation, or anything, just explore. When you explore, you learn. As I write this book, I am 25 years old and this is the age where Indian parents are at their most alert level when it comes to marriage. Most of my school friends and college mates have got married and are looking forward to living a life of "happily ever after". While I am happy for each one of them and may God bless their relationships. However, conversely, I meet people who believe that they are engineers, they need a partner who choose the same field as them. If they are a doctor, they need a doctor and if they are high profile professional, they need someone of similar standards. Well, there is nothing wrong with any of these. It's all about your perception of what you desire from life. If those needs are met, you are good to go ahead in life. But, if you do not explore the wider perspective, how would you know life? How would you know what's in store for you? In the movie Dear Zindagi, Shah Rukh Khan says, *"When we go out for furniture shopping, we try out various chairs to see which is more comfortable and authentic. Then why don't we explore different people when it comes to life partners"*. It's not only about life partners but in every area of your life, just explore. Learn something new and unique and who knows in the process, you might find something more meaningful. But if you don't explore, you never know!

I have applied this principle in my life. Today, I try to learn and explore all areas of my life. I meet a wide variety of people, go out to places I have never been before, try different flavors of life, read books I once thought made no sense to me, make new friends in unknown places, and understand different perspectives. I keep exploring. And I suggest you keep exploring as well. Let me repeat this again, "**When you explore, you learn. When you learn, you understand various patterns. When you understand various patterns, you analyze life and once you start analyzing life, you become self-aware. In order to become self-aware about your likes and dislikes, you must first explore**".

"*Life is not about traveling from point A to point B. It's about exploring all the alphabets and choosing which alphabet(s) set your soul on fire*"

CHAPTER ELEVEN

You have all the Answers

*#innerwisdom #innertransformation
#universe #meditation #spirituality
#higherself #justthebeginning
#perception #reframemind
#transformation #reprogramlife*

For the first 23 years of my life, I was like a child wandering all around, trying to grab hold of everything in life and whenever anything slipped away from me, I used to constantly ask questions to God "Why did this occur to me?" I remember the 1st sports tournament I lost when I was 10 years old. I remember the 1st time I ever flunked my examinations. I remember the 1st time I was ever criticized in public. I remember my 1st major failure in life and I remember my 1st ever heartbreak in life. All these circumstances had two things in common

- I used to sob for hours together.

- Look up and ask God "Why me?"

- As humans, we do have the tendency to ask God, "Why me?", whenever things don't go our way. Although, at the back of our minds, we do know that failures are part and parcel of our life and we should face them with courage, *AND MOST IMPORTANTLY, LEARN FROM FAILURES*. We all know this lesson, yet we all act like babies from time to time, don't we? In 2020, when I took 100% responsibility for my life, I decided to ask more questions. I needed to understand myself and my failures. I was in search of answers. I asked my parents and my best friends, who had seen my life in and out. I constantly raised questions such as:

- Why did this occur to me?
- Why did I fail?
- Why did I become such a pathetic student?
- How did I lose my momentum in life?
- How and when did I start losing interest in sports?
- Why didn't I speak up when I was in pain?
- What happened to me?
- What happened to that old Meghana who used to enjoy life and help others?
- When did I change?
- Why did I change?
- When did I start being a dishonest person?
- When did my life turn negative?

Now, remember these are the questions I raised when I was broken and shattered in life. To my surprise, my parents and friends did their best to help me out in finding answers but none of the advice helped me 100 percent. My heart couldn't agree with anyone and I was confused, and at the same time curious in search of answers. I needed more.

One morning I came across a quote that said "The answers are always on the inside". It was an eye-opening moment. It was one of those moments when your intuition yells at you saying "Hey, this one is for you". My immediate question was "What do you mean by inside?". I read a couple of self-help and spiritual books to wrap my head around this concept of 'inside'. It's only after 3 months of consistent meditation practices, I started to get answers during my meditation, in my dreams, and in the form of books. All of a sudden, I felt someone is directing me during my meditation or my dreams are answering my questions and the books I read, are all of a sudden talking to me. Every time I received the answers, I used to yell happily saying Oh My God! Within a span of 6 months, all my intense questions about my previous failures were answered. I felt a sense of relief but I had more questions to ask. This time, deeper, meaningful and intense questions about life. Thus, my daily chore of meditation became a source through which I would communicate and receive from God, the universe and angels. I became so addicted to mediation, praying and talking to my imaginary friends that I didn't realize I was on a path of spirituality.

All my life, I was seeking answers to my questions from the external world. But little did I know that the internal world, the inner self and the inner wisdom are a source of infinite intelligence. Some people call this the higher self or intuition but you can call it anything you like. Once you realize and firmly believe that the answers you are searching for, are inside of you, the universe will respond to your questions. From my experience, I can firmly state that you have all the answers within you. You have an entire library within you. You have an entire Wikipedia inside you. You have Google inside you. You have YouTube, Instagram and Facebook inside you and more importantly, you have the entire universe inside you. **Tune into yourself and let the universal energy respond to your questions.**

Accept the light within you
and...

You will light up the world

Here are some of my daily rituals that can help you connect to your higher self:

Meditation – Meditation is one of the most powerful techniques that can help you become physically, mentally, emotionally, and spiritually well balanced. It has a calming effect on your mind which can then help you connect to your higher self. When I started my meditation journey, I could sit barely for 5 minutes. I understand the initial days are difficult but that's the breakthrough you need in order to experience the benefits later on.

Journaling – This is another powerful technique that can help you understand yourself better. Often people misjudge by thinking journaling is all about jotting down daily activities, but it's more than that. Journaling is therapeutic, it's a conversation with yourself, and it's a self-reflection technique. Journaling can help you develop self-awareness which can then assist you to connect to your higher self by asking the right deep questions. All you need to do is, take some time out, sit in a noise-free comfortable environment along with your journal, and finally start asking questions about any incident that's been bothering you. Remember – While journaling one must be open-minded, and non-judgemental either towards oneself or others. Then ask more questions. The more you ask questions and go deeper within, one day you will find the answers.

Seek Help – This is one of the practices that can help you feel lighter. Sometimes we are flooded with our own negative thoughts and we end up taking decisions based on emotions rather than using our logical minds. Thus seeking help either from a professional, family member or friends can help you see things clearly, especially during the initial days. Talk to anyone whom you trust and share a strong bond with. Sometimes venting out the baggage we carry over our shoulders can help us go within ourselves to find more meaningful answers.

Be Open– When we are over-involved in finding answers to our problems, we tend to think about them all the time and thus build resistance- I might get my answer from XYZ practice only. I request you to be open to all the practices because you never know how the answers might come to you, the universe speaks in mysterious ways. Reading books has certainly helped me get answers to some deep meaningful questions about life. Always remember, when we are curious enough to find answers, the universe might direct us towards a certain book or we might accidentally come across a random author or a podcast or a video or a billboard, etc. Pay attention to these signs, they are directing you towards something you asked for.

Thank you – One of the most effective and easy techniques. When you are on the journey towards inner exploration, thank you can work wonders. When you express gratitude to the power that's greater than you, you send a message and vibration out there that you firmly believe your answers are on the way. You are directly connecting and commanding your higher self for the answers- in a more loving and compassionate way.

I hope these techniques will help you connect to your higher self. One pro tip- Do not worry about WHEN and HOW the answers will come to you, just continue your practices, and whenever you are ready, trust me, the answers WILL arrive.

As I conclude this book, it's been almost 2 years since I unknowingly embarked on a journey of spirituality. It's been a phenomenal journey so far and I can't wait to see what's more in store for me. I look back at life when I was 23 years old, broke, filled with rage and insecurity. I was directionless and had no mission in life. Today, I am a person who is at peace with myself, filled with joy and contentment. As I spread my wings wide apart, my heart swells as I express gratitude to the supreme God, the universe, the angelic and spiritual realm and my higher self, who are constantly guiding me, supporting me and helping me inspire others.

Let my transformational story inspire you to take action. Always remember, *you are born for a reason, you are unique and you have a purpose in this lifetime. You have a miraculous light within you and a higher source of energy that's constantly guiding you. You have all the answers inside you - make sure you tune into your higher self on a daily basis because my dear,* **your presence is a gift to the world.**

This is just the beginning. Signing off, until our paths cross again in the future.

More Power to You!

Books Recommendation

- The Power of your subconscious mind by Dr. Joseph Murphy.
- Life's amazing secrets by Gaur Gopal Das.
- The universe has your back by Gabreille Bernstein.
- Super attractor by Gabrielle Bernstein.
- Attitude is Everything by Jeff Keller.
- Start with why by Simon Sinek.
- The surrender experiment by Michael A Singer.
- Think and grow rich by Napoleon Hill.
- Winning by Tim S Grover.
- Good vibes, good life by Vex king.
- Atomic habits by James Clear.
- Think like a monk by Jay Shetty.
- Master your emotions by Thibaut Meurisse.
- Limitless by Jim Kwik.
- Ikigai by Hector Garcia and Francesc.
- The Alchemist by Paulo Coelho
- The Secret by Rhoda Byrne.
- Do epic shit by Ankur Warikoo.

... The ultimate and the most powerful life guide
"BHAGAVAD-GITA"

Thank You!

There are many incredible souls who helped me bring this book to life. I am forever grateful to have spoken to Kunal Trehan, who entered my life as a Guardian angel and planted the seed of publishing the book. Thank you Dhiraj Ranjan, who's been on this journey with me from the very beginning. I am deeply grateful to all my best friends- Vinay, Manasvi, Pradnya, Devika, and Jyoti, thank you so much for constantly believing in me. A huge shout-out to my mom, dad, and bro for constantly tolerating my melodrama and supporting me in all my endeavors. I thank the entire WeTalk Team for their work!

Finally, I thank you, my reader, for taking out your precious time to get on this roller coaster ride with Edit Life. I hope this book radiates unconditional love and reminds you that your presence is a GIFT to the world.

With lots of love
Meghana Kulkarni

About The Author

Meghana Kulkarni is a Former Professional Athlete, an Electrical Engineer, a Mindset Mentor, and a Healer. She is the host of a podcast called ATHLETE MIND. Obsessed with Personal development and fascinated by the power of mind and spirituality, her life mission is to help professional athletes enhance their performance by enhancing their mindset by combining the art of science and spirituality. Her ultimate mission is to raise and expand the level of consciousness on planet earth. For more on Meghana's work, please visit www.meghanakulkarni.com